RHOADS' WEST

TO JOHN HUFF

MEET YOU AT
MAUDE'S PLACE!

BEST WISHES,

FRED
RHOADS

RHOADS'

" I HOPE YOU DIDN'T BUY
A ROUND TRIP TICKET, LADY! "

WEST

FRED RHOADS

By Fred Rhoads

Foreword by Ben K. Green

Northland Press / Flagstaff, Arizona

To my son Fred who loves the old West if it was only air conditioned.

FOREWORD

THE WEST HAS BEEN PORTRAYED in many ways — historically, artistically, rightfully, and wrongfully. It is flat refreshing to see the way Fred Rhoads takes a humorous look at this sometimes misunderstood and often misrepresented Western way of life.

I have been known to be a darn hard critic when it comes to anything about horses, be it in the flesh, the written word, or painted on canvas. In an awful lot of cases I feel my criticisms have well been justified. Too many artists make a horse look humorous, though unintentionally. Fred Rhoads makes humorous horses, funny people, and laughable cartoons. He's intentional.

For many years you have been amused by Fred Rhoads' cartoons but in different surroundings—mainly a little army character named Sad Sack, who has entertained people throughout the world. As a professional gag-writer and cartoonist, Fred Rhoads has not only been writing and drawing Sad Sack, for Harvey

Feature Syndicate, but also has collaborated on two other famous cartoon characters, Beetle Bailey and Snuffy Smith.

When Fred first moved West to Tucson, Arizona his humorous, but jaundiced eye, caught a glance of the so-called West and this series of cartoons started coming off his boards.

Fred Rhoads' cartoons possess the rare quality of bringing laughs to the Western people that they are drawn about. Many cartoons demand extra long captions, practically explanations, for anyone to even guess what they are trying to portray. Not the case in *Rhoads' West* where at first glance the humor takes full rein.

The pride we all have in our Western heritage, as well as present day-by-day happenings, has been caught by the humorous and stylish pen of Fred Rhoads. I'm sure you'll enjoy as much as I have — traveling *Rhoads' West.*

BEN K. GREEN

INTRODUCTION

ALTHOUGH I ONLY DO humorous drawings of the dusty cowboys and earthy characters out of the Old West, since I'm a cartoonist — it's the one way I can express how stirring I feel those times really were.

Now, speaking of stirring. Put together a bunch of saddle tramp cowboys, wagon trains, six shooters, cattle drives, U.S. Cavalry, gold bonanzas, Indian raids, ladies of leisure, buffalo skinners, gamblers, silver strikes, and renegade Indians with Cochise and Geronimo thrown in! Mix them all up and you'll see what I mean about stirring times!

Anyway, with all the shoot-outs, cattle rustlings, hangings, boozing, horse thieving, knifings, bank robbers, poison arrows, crooked sheriffs, rattlesnakes, bounty hunters, dandruff, card sharks, claim jumpers, bad breath, gold mine salting, dust storms, dance hall girls, blizzards, holdup men, back stabbing,

athlete's feet, and drunken brawls, there must have been some-
thing that kept those people going.

Maybe they had a sense of humor. . . .

FRED RHOADS

P.S. Come to think of it, the West hasn't changed much.

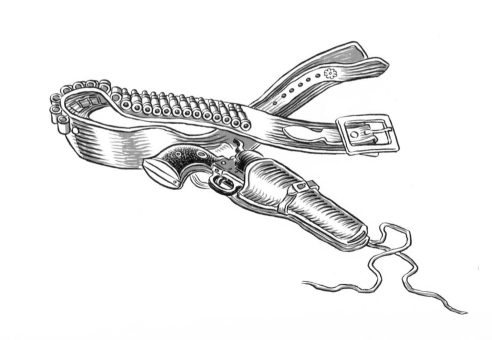

"I THINK IT'S GOING TO RAIN........
MY CORNS ACHE AND I HEAR THUNDER!"

"THE RIVER SHOULD BE ALONG ANY MINUTE NOW!"

"A HELLUVA SPOT YOU PICKED TO BUILD A TOWN!
.......THIS IS THE CHISHOLM TRAIL!"

"HELL! WE'RE ALL SCARED, LADY! YOU'LL JUST HAVE TO HOLD IT LIKE EVERYBODY ELSE!"

FRED
RHOADS

"I THOUGHT THIS WAS THE SHORT CUT EAST!"

"I THOUGHT THIS WAS THE SHORT CUT WEST!"

"BEFORE YOU HIGH-TAIL IT OUT OF HERE,
WOULD YOU GIVE ME YOUR AUTOGRAPH?"

"COMPANY HALT!"

"THAT REMINDS ME, I'VE GOT TO WORK
IN THE STOCKYARDS TOMORROW!"

FRED
RHOads

" THESE INDIANS HAVE TO LEARN
TO LIVE LIKE DECENT AMERICANS!
SHOOT EVERY DAMN ONE OF THEM! "

" IF I SIT DOWN, WE'LL NEVER GET THE REVOLUTION OFF THE GROUND! "

FRED
RHOADS

"WHICH WAY TO THE BANK, MISTER ?
WE'RE INTERESTED IN A WITHDRAWAL!"

"YES, PARSON! MY HIRED HANDS ALWAYS OBSERVE THIS AS A DAY OF REST!"

"I DON'T KNOW IF YOU CAUGHT IT FROM THE HORSES,
OR THE HORSES CAUGHT IT FROM YOU!"

"GET OFF MY BACK!"

"I WISH THIS MOMENT COULD LAST FOREVER!"

"I'M GLAD YOU BUSTED IN HERE, SHERIFF!
I COULDN'T HAVE HELD OFF THIS HOSTILE
INDIAN SAVAGE ANOTHER SECOND!"

"I AM NOT A COWARD, SIR! I JUST REMEMBERED MY FURLOUGH STARTS TODAY!"

"I DON'T CARE IF YOU'VE GOT A COLD OR NOT ....JUST DON'T SNEEZE!"

"I THINK WE FOUND A GOOD PLACE
TO SPEND THE NIGHT.
RIGHT NEXT TO THIS BABBLING BROOK!"

"WE SHEEPMEN NEED A STEADY-FINGERED GUNMAN! WHERE'S THE MAN THEY CALL "STRAIGHT SHOT"?"

"I FIXED THAT ROOF TODAY.....WHY IS IT LEAKING?"

"COULD I BORROW A DRINK OF WATER ?
.... ABOUT 2000 GALLONS!"

"I KNOW YOU'RE NOT SCARED
IN THIS GHOST TOWN, KILLER, BUT WHY DO YOU
ALWAYS SLEEP IN THE MIDDLE?"

"THIS LOOKS LIKE A GOOD ONE......
DANG! I WISH I COULD READ!"

"NOW THAT'S WHAT I CALL FANCY....... A ROOM AND BATH!"

"DAG NAB IT! THAT BATH I TOOK IN THAT HOTEL WAS A PURE WASTE!"

" YOU CAN'T HAVE FOUR ACES, 'CAUSE
I'VE GOT FIVE ACES!.....YOU MUST BE CHEATIN'! "

"I'VE BEEN PUSHIN' THESE STEERS AND EATIN' DUST FOR TWO MONTHS! THEY CAN'T SAY I HAVEN'T BEEN KEEPIN' MY MIND ON THESE BEERS....I MEAN STEERS!"

"BEFORE WE LEFT THE RANCH,
DID YOU MILK THOSE COWS?"

FRED
RHOADS

"LET'S SEE .... WHAT'S ON THE MENU?"

FRED
RHOADS

" A FINANCIAL RUT?......THIS RANCH IS
IN A RUT ANYWAY YOU LOOK AT IT! "

"DO YOU HAVE TO TAP YOUR FINGER LIKE THAT?"

"IT'LL BE GOOD TO GET BACK ON THE TRAIL.
THIS CITY LIFE MAKES YOU SOFT!"

"EVERYTHING AROUND HERE
IS STARTIN' TO SAG!"

"WELL, BACK TO THE OLD HANG OUT!"

"IT SURE IS DROPPING OUT HERE TOO!"

"GET MARRIED ?!! DURN!
YOU CAUGHT ME WITH MY PANTS DOWN!"

"----AND DO YOU, MADAM,-----"

FRED
RHOADS

"WE'RE OFF TO A GOOD START, MAUDE.
WE'VE GOT A HOUSE!"

"I'VE HAD IT WITH YOU, MAUDE.
WE'VE HAD TOO MANY FALLING OUTS!"

"DANG! IT'S SCRAMBLED EGGS AGAIN!"

FRED
RHOADS

"SHUCKS! THIS IS NOTHIN', KID.
ONE TIME I WAS SO BUSY SHOOTIN' INDIANS WITH BOTH HANDS,
I HAD TO ROLL ONE WITH MY TOES!"

" YOU'RE BEAUTIFUL AND I'M NOT SAYIN' THAT
JUST BECAUSE I HAD TWENTY BEERS
AND YOU'RE THE ONLY WOMAN WITHIN 200 MILES! "

"YOU SAVE TWO DAYS, BUT YOU AGE TWO YEARS!"

"THEN IT'S AGREED THAT WE ABSOLUTELY REFUSE TO
EAT ANYMORE OF THAT COOK'S ROTTEN COOKIN'----"

COME AN'
GET IT!

"DESERT, MY FOOT! WE'RE CROSSING
THE RIVER GRANDEOSO!"

"SA-AAY! WE HAVEN'T HAD FLAPJACKS IN A LONG TIME!"

"YEP! THAT FORTUNE TELLER WAS RIGHT..... SHE SAID
HE WAS DUE FOR A TRIP AND A BIG BREAK! "

"ICE CREAM ?!
IT'LL TAKE TWO WEEKS TO GET ANY
ICE CREAM ! "

" NOW YOU'LL NOT ONLY **HANG**, YOU'LL ALSO GET **TEN YEARS** FOR DESTROYING GOVERNMENT PROPERTY! "

"I'M THE FASTEST GUN IN THE -----AG--GGGH!"

FRED
RHOADS

"CRABBY'S ALWAYS MOANING ABOUT HIS PAY!
.... HERE'S WHERE HE GETS A RAISE!"

"I'LL BE ALL RIGHT AS LONG AS YOU KEEP TALKING TO ME!"

" I JUST REMEMBERED THAT NEW GIRL'S NAME
I MET IN TOWN LAST NIGHT...........FANNY! "

"JUST ONCE, I WISH HE'D SAY GENTLEMEN, THE BAR IS CLOSED!"

PALACE SALOON

FRED
RHOADS

"I ALREADY GAVE HIM COD LIVER OIL, BLACK STRAP MOLASSES, SNAKE OIL AND BOILED CACTUS ROOT! WHAT DOES HE NEED A DOCTOR FOR?"

"I SURE WILL BE GLAD
WHEN THE DROUGHT'S OVER!"

EVERYTHING ALWAYS COMES OUT
ALL RIGHT IN THE END